Self-Regulation Workbook for Teens

Say Goodbye to Stress, Anxiety, Anger Bursts, and Uncontrolled Crying, and Experience Your New Life Full of Joy, Emotional Balance, Connection, and Self-Acceptance

Emma Wills

Table of Contents

Introduction

Emotions, how you deal with them, and their impact on you are important. Many people stop their lives because depression takes away their desire to move forward; some break off relationships or lifelong friendships because anger makes them say unforgivable words.

This workbook will help you work on your emotions and self-regulation.

What Is Self-Regulation?

Self-regulation is a personal skill that allows you to set goals and move toward them. Therefore, it is a self-directed process. It is also an essential skill for environmental adaptation and adequate personal and social adjustment. If you want to know what it is to regulate emotions and how to do it, you are in the right book.

What does self-regulation mean? Self-regulation is essential for you to adapt to situations and act following your goals. Below, I will delve deeper into this topic.

Why Is Self-Regulation Important for Adolescents?

Emotional self-regulation in adolescents is a core component of emotional intelligence because it involves developing the ability to manage your feelings, whether they are pleasant or painful, rather than being ruled by them.

Emotional self-control has to do with the ability to keep your emotions within a certain adaptive range in the face of what is happening.

Having emotional self-control means that you are aware of your feelings, express them, and know how to manage them appropriately.

I know that emotions guide and condition behavior; for example, if you are angry, worried, or tense, you find it hard to sit down and learn a class, and the behavior limits you too much.

If you can't regulate your emotions, you won't be able to control your behavior.

Behavioral problems in adolescents are often related to difficulty regulating emotions appropriately.

Why Will This Workbook Help You Manage Stress, Anxiety, Anger, and Crying?

In this book, you will have tools in each of the chapters so you can deal with stress, which is something that is part of all people because when an episode does not go well, or we are engaged, as in a difficult math test that will define whether we will pass the subject or not, we feel a lot of stress. The point is to know how to regulate it.

Anxiety is another of the problems that follow unchanneled stress since you can start with a feeling of great stress, which is not called that, but anxiety, or go to the extreme and feel a kind of great fear; these are anxiety attacks. You can also feel anger, uncontrollable anger where you want to explode everything or even cry. You feel those immense desires to burst into tears with intensity until you empty yourself because you have a lot of sadness.

It is partly normal to feel this, but it is also important that you know how to control it, live it, and overcome it; this book will help you to achieve it.

The process of achieving emotional self-regulation begins in the first months of life and continues into adulthood. Each child follows their path to emotional maturity; some arrive quickly, while others take more work. In this process of emotional and behavioral self-regulation, there are several aspects of influence.

Temperament is a determining factor in regulating emotions from a young age. Some babies are more sensitive and intense in emotions, such as feeling bad, and find it more difficult to calm down, while other kids, in the same situation, act softer and are easier to calm down.

The environment plays an important role in the acquisition of emotional self-regulation: It has to do with the parent's role as an external regulator. When children are young, parents provide role models for how to react to and manage emotions, especially those that create discomfort or frustration.

Emotional dysregulation involves difficulty managing our emotions and behavior, manifested by experiencing intense emotions and difficulty returning to a calm state.

In all cases, the priority is to be aware that emotions such as anger, frustration, or fear are natural and that the ways in which they are displayed are inappropriate, such as destructive behavior towards others or yourself.

It is essential to learn to reflect on the consequences of impulsive reactions.

Different approaches are used to learn to manage emotions and behavior, such as emotion-focused behavior management techniques, play techniques, and relaxation techniques.

When children are very young, mainly play techniques (play, storytelling, drawing) are used to regulate emotions and behavior. In addition, interventions focus on the need to provide orientation and guidance to parents to help them find effective ways to address their children's behavioral problems.

Older children use tools such as the ones you will see here.

How to Use This Book

You can get the most out of this book by consciously taking each chapter, reading the exercises, and putting them into action with concentration and as I recommend. Also, by placing in your mind the commitment that you will heal and improve, and take better care of your emotions with a more focused emotional intelligence.

Let's begin this journey of chapters to understand our emotions better.

Chapter #1: Emotional Umbrella

Imagine you are somewhere, and you have an umbrella over you, emotions fall on it, all of them, and they splash you a little; if you take it away, you will get soaked; if you leave it, you will get a little wet. Think about the size of that umbrella; maybe you will get some drops or get very wet.

Know the common emotions and what triggers them, the healthy and not-so-healthy emotions, and learn to identify them, sure many times you have felt something, but it is not sadness; you have exploded in anger, but... you did not feel so angry, or you also had sadness and frustration. Let's see it and understand it.

Common Emotions and Their Triggers

Emotions are about one of the mental processes that reflect a person's attitude toward himself and the world around him. They have a great relationship with two sciences: psychology and biology.

Emotions are experiences you have at a certain moment. The intensity of the experience depends on the importance of the situation you are living in.

But in addition to the experience, there is also a psychological component, as well as the biological element, certain physiological changes that happen in the body parallel to the experience.

Anger

Anger is one of the strongest emotions you can experience, and is described as a feeling of resentment or anger at having been offended or wronged.

It is energetic, explosive, and often unruly. As the name implies, it is a feeling of intense dissatisfaction and unhappiness. The difficulty with anger is that it is multifaceted.

It can range from mild discomfort to intense anger. If not managed properly, the consequences can be severe. It can destroy your relationships and cause problems in your personal and professional life.

Anger, on the other hand, can be very constructive. It can help you let go and motivates you to move forward when you feel insecure about life, as long as that anger is not directed at the person who hurt you.

Happiness

Happiness is the emotion you probably seek the most; everyone does. Although people experience happiness for different reasons, emotion is defined as a pleasurable feeling of contentment, happiness, and well-being.

Psychology today is as concerned with helping others find joy as it was about 50 years ago. However, there is a strong relationship between physical and mental health. To be happy, you must take care of both your body and your mind.

Disgust

Seen from the evolutionary side, disgust is a way of looking at something you like or dislike; for example, you see a plate with delicious food and another with maggots boiling in the meat—yuck! It can be defined as a feeling of repulsion caused by something offensive and unpleasant.

You can feel it both physically and mentally, as it can cause intense physical sensations and severe emotional imbalance. You feel sick to your stomach and want to vomit.

Sadness

Sadness is something that many people go through. It is defined as a limited space of hopelessness or disappointment. If you feel it too often, it can become a chronic depression.

The intensity and duration change according to what triggers it and your individual characteristics.

Surprise

Surprise is the brief shock that follows an unexpected event. It is usually very intense and can be defined as a feeling of unhappiness or pain or the opposite.

Studies have shown that people tend to remember surprises for a long time because they are different from everyday situations.

Surprise can trigger the same response as fear.

Fear

One of the most important emotions you have, fear is a form of worry that is usually triggered by the perception or feeling of pain, danger, or threat.

It is understood as an unpleasant emotion that follows a perceived danger or threat, such as when you are walking home and are startled by a large dog that looks like it will bite you.

When you are afraid, your brain goes into fight-or-flight mode, then your senses intensify, and your heart rate accelerates. Of course, we all respond to danger differently, and the level of fear you experience can be measured by how you feel, depending on many factors.

Difference Between Healthy and Unhealthy Emotions

About what this subtitle says, I want to give a quick answer, there are two types of emotions: healthy and unhealthy. That's why I made this subdivision, so you learn to differentiate them and so you know the first step to the path you should follow, knowing whether what you feel is good or not.

Most people experience positive emotions easily and even tend to think that they are the only ones they can have. But the reality is that negative emotions happen too. When they come, you probably want them to go away as soon as possible, you tend to feel like the unluckiest person in the world, and you don't know what to do with what you are feeling.

In What Unhealthy Ways Do We React?

Responding too aggressively will not make the negative emotions disappear but will worsen the situation.

Acting in a passive-avoidant way, i.e., running away from episodes that cause your emotions to trigger other negative feelings, such as guilt or depression.

Blocking, becoming paralyzed.

These are ways to deal with emotions in a bad way, but the most important point is that you learn to distinguish between the healthy and the harmful and try to do it with a very simple exercise to apply at the end of the day, about what you feel or what you live in that moment.

What Are Healthy Negative Emotions?

A healthy negative emotion is characterized by its shorter duration (hours or days), which is when you need to find a solution to overcome it. It will not stop you or make you run away, but you will get through these situations. In the end, the intensity is appropriate to the situation in which it is provoked.

For their part, the main characteristic of unhealthy negative emotions is that they last for a long time, weeks, or months. They can cause exhaustion and, at the same time, emotional disorders because their intensity does not correspond to what is happening.

Worry is a negative emotion that manifests itself when you feel stressed in a situation, and to know if it is healthy or not, you should consider the following factors.

It would be healthy if it was a real stress for me or my family, as it was when we tested negative on those medical tests.

Then, suppose the worry arises from our cognitive rigidity (wanting to control everything). In that case, it is considered unhealthy because you want the situation to be perfect and safe, or like when you are constantly worried about whether your family members are sick or in traffic jams.

Sadness occurs when you experience loss or alienation from a person or situation. Feeling sad is healthy if that loss or distance is objectively present. An example is if you move to another city and have to say goodbye to family and friends temporarily.

Sadness would not be healthy if there was no real distance or loss, or if there was, but the grief has lived with you for a long time and with very high intensity. For example, if you are sad because your partner did not call you today, or if you have long since moved to another city, you cannot build a new life there because the feeling of homesickness remains with you.

Shame arises when you think you are showing your worst mistakes or flaws. It would be healthy if you fell on the steps at school or were at karaoke and lots of people saw you, and laugh at you, but it would not be beneficial if you eliminate physical contact or stop doing things you loved because of shame, like sunbathing or enjoying people.

Regret is a negative emotion that arises when you break the rules, and it can be healthy if the rules you start with are consistent, i.e., not perfectionistic or rigid. This emotion can arise, for example, if you forget to bring a gift you promised a friend, or miss school and say you were sick when you were actually on a trip. It would not be healthy if you go on for a long time and are always thinking about it, or if there is no objective reason, such as constantly worrying about whether a friend is angry with you when you are not arguing or not giving money to someone in the street.

Anger is just about the most common negative emotion. It occurs when you feel that someone or something is an external threat or danger to you or your loved ones or when someone does something you don't like. Healthy anger is when someone insults you and wants you to feel inferior or if you get a grade lowered for no reason. On the other hand, unhealthy anger occurs when that feeling remains because of a past situation; that is when it is interpreted as if other people have genuine intentions to hurt. An example would be if someone stands in front of you in line at the store thinking or believing that you are stupid and will not notice, or if you get home and the internet is not working, and you are filled with anger even though you have other options.

How to Identify and Label Your Own Emotions

Emotion labeling is a mechanism by which people attempt to identify emotions in themselves or others using specific words. That is, in this verbal situation, what you do is label a very specific emotion you are experiencing or you intuitively believe the other person is experiencing.

This transcendental action may seem very obvious and simple, but it is essential because it first allows the translation of sometimes very deep and complex emotions into your spoken language, which helps you understand them and how you should feel.

These labels are also fundamental to sharing such information, that is, to transmit to another person what you are experiencing, sometimes in a simple word. You say it, and others understand you immediately. By sharing what you feel, you make it clear that you are angry at that moment for X reason, and that you need a minute.

But beyond this basic (but crucial) utility, the reality is that emotion labels have deeper meanings, which I'll show you below.

If you've been going through a lot of lows lately, or find yourself dealing with a negative event affecting your mood, the best thing to do is to see a psychologist, a professional who can help you talk to understand how you feel and know how to do it. By working with an expert, you can control those volatile emotions. In milder cases, perhaps what psychologists call "emotional labeling," that mechanism that serves to identify your emotions and those of others so that you know how to handle them better, will help you see in others what they feel right now.

The first of these emotion labeling utilities that I want you to see is precisely that of emotion regulation. As I have already mentioned, by identifying emotions in words, you can become aware of your state of mind.

This skill opens the door to another very interesting possibility: emotional regulation. And by being aware of your emotions, you can learn to control what you feel if they are too strong and cause discomfort for any other reason.

The first point is that you take the emotional labeling, then use it to become aware of the specific emotion you are experiencing, and finally, employ this knowledge to process the emotion in question, managing to reduce the level of intensity or even replace it with another one.

If you use it correctly, this skill can serve you on a therapeutic level as a resource to treat various conditions, such as phobias.

Katharina Kircanski and her collaborators studied this phenomenon in a 2012 book. This research involved the use of emotional labels to help people with an extreme fear of spiders. Two groups were formed for this purpose. Both used the technique of exposure to the aversive stimulus to treat their phobias, i.e., that the spider filled them with panic.

However, one of the groups also had another variable applied to them: the label of the emotion they were feeling at the time. After a week of the study, the researchers came to a different conclusion. There appeared to be no significant difference in the level of fear the participants said they experienced.

Interestingly, however, the group that, in addition to being exposed to the spiders, also worked with emotional labels trying to express exactly how they felt, showed lower physiological responses to the aversive stimulus (spider) after the treatment compared to the control group. The response was measured by skin conductance.

It was also found that individuals in the experimental group could approach spiders more easily than those who did not use language to express their feelings and emotions during the treatment phase, i.e., those who did not use emotion labels.

The main conclusion Kircanski and colleagues found in the study was that using more words to try to define exactly what they were feeling seemed to help participants in the experimental group reduce their fear.

This effect is interesting and deserves further study, as the data suggest that emotional labeling may be a powerful ally in healing phobias and that this effect could be used to help patients with other mental illnesses.

Exercise: what are the emotions you feel most often that scare you the most? What pleasant feelings do you want to experience most often?

Here are ways to better understand your emotions:

Notice your emotions and name them. First, see how you feel when things happen to you. Talk about your inner emotions. Do you feel proud when things go well? Or disappointed if you do poorly on a test? Can you feel relaxed when you sit down with friends for lunch? Or nervous before a test?

Tracking Emotions

Choose an emotion, such as joy, and track that mood throughout the day. Notice how often you feel that way. Maybe you are happy when something good happens, or you are happy when a friend comes to visit. You may feel happy when someone offers to help you or says something nice about you. Or you're just glad it's Friday. Write in your mind or on a piece of paper each time you feel happy. Is it a mild, medium, or very strong emotion?

Learn new vocabulary for emotions. How many different emotions can you name? Try to think of a few more.

How many anger words do you know? For example, you may feel frustrated, annoyed, or angry. You may also be angry, irritated, or enraged.

Write an emotion journal. Take a few minutes daily to write down how you feel and why. Writing down what you feel will help you understand them better.

You can make crafts, write poems or compose songs to express your emotions.

Identifying emotions in works of art, songs, and movies is another option. Look at what the artist does to express what he or she feels. What do you think of his or her work?

Take a moment to understand your emotions better. Just pay attention to how you feel. Accept how you are, and don't judge yourself. Be good to yourself.

Remember that all emotions are normal. But how you act on them is very important. When you understand your feelings, you can make informed decisions about how to act, no matter how you feel.

How to Increase Emotions

Start by Increasing Positive Emotions

Identify the positive emotions you want to increase. Let's say you want to be more cheerful. Think of different situations or activities that might have produced this emotion. Write down as much as you can.

Focus on something small and simple, like a song that makes you happy when you hear it. Each time you feel happy, add to the list the situation or activity that makes you feel that way.

Once you know what triggers the emotions you want to increase, you can decide how to incorporate these activities into your daily routine. Choose things that make sense to do each day. You may not be able to take a walk on the beach, but when you hear a song that reminds you of summer vacation, you'll feel happy.

Commit to taking one or more actions to boost the feeling you want to increase in your life. Make time for these experiences. This emotional exercise is equivalent to the recommended 5 daily servings of fruits and vegetables, as they will protect your mental health.

Create a Positive Experience Collection

Sometimes you may forget how to hit your positive emotions. You may need a reminder to get back to that happy place. To do this, a collection of positive experiences is helpful.

These collections of experiences remind you and make you feel the good times in your life, the things you are good at, the joys and accomplishments, the things that make you happy, the music you like, the people you love, or what you want. It's a collection of positivity.

Collect items that emotionally take you back to another time in your life. For example:

Some writing or drawing you created.

Favorite quotes that inspire you or the lyrics of a favorite song.

Photos or memories of joyful moments.

A photo of someone you admire.

Awards that remind you of triumphs.

Memories from your childhood.

Cards or written comments from key people in your life.

A gift someone has given you.

Put everything in a special folder or box that you can easily access. You can also use these collections to create collages, posters, or moving sculptures. The most important point is to choose elements that generate positive emotions in you. You can add, delete or change parts at any time.

When you are sad or depressed, take a few minutes to look at this collection and recharge yourself with positive emotions. Watch it anytime for daily positivity.

When you work to increase your positive emotions, you may find that you are happier, accomplish more and have more energy. A small amount of focused, positive investment daily will pay off in the long run.

Chapter #2: Toolbox

This is a toolbox for you to pull out when you feel you are facing situations and don't know if you are doing it right or not; in the end, my plan is for you to learn how to face them correctly. After I give you a set of tools, I will explain what mindfulness is and how mindfulness is used.

Difference Between Healthy and Unhealthy Coping Strategies and How to Recognize Them

Coping strategies are actions you take, either consciously or unconsciously, to deal with stress, problems, or uncomfortable emotions. Unhealthy coping strategies often feel good at the moment, but they will leave consequences over time. Healthy coping strategies may not bring you instant gratification, but they lead to lasting positive results.

Examples of Unhealthy Coping Strategies

Drug or alcohol use

Overeating

Procrastinating

Sleeping too much or too little

Social isolation

Self-injury

Aggression

Examples of Healthy Coping Strategies

Exercising

Talking about problems

Eating healthy

Getting professional help

Relaxation techniques (e.g., deep breathing)

Use of social supports

Problem-solving techniques

Sample Situations

Bella had to turn in a research paper on one of the subjects. Because the paper was so demanding, she felt anxious every time she thought about the deadline. When she distracted herself from other activities, she felt better. Bella used procrastination as a coping strategy to avoid anxiety. This helped her feel better, but it could cause problems in the long run.

Billy felt jealous whenever his girlfriend spent time with her friends. Trying to control the situation, he belittled his girlfriend's friends in an abusive manner and asked her to stay home. When Billy's girlfriend agreed to what he asked, he was relieved. Billy used aggression to cope with the situation and avoid the discomfort of jealousy.

Rebecca feels anger because she didn't get the best grade in school. Instead of talking to her parents or another teacher about it and trying to improve her school performance, she continued to hold on to her anger. Later, Rebecca learned to control her anger by drinking. Alcohol temporarily calms Rebecca's anger, but the problems at school remain unresolved.

How to Develop Healthy Coping Strategies

Anger, pity, anger, fear: We've all experienced these uncomfortable, sometimes unbearable emotions. Painful emotions are part of being human, and learning how to respond to them healthily and sustainably is one of the most important lessons you can learn.

One of the best ways to help you cope with strong emotions is to develop healthy coping skills, such as practices you can use to reduce the intensity or frequency of unwanted emotions. Different people may need different coping skills, but here are some examples of safe and effective actions that are often helpful in stressful situations:

Seek sensory stimulation, such as splashing cold water on your face or holding ice cubes.

Writing a journal.

Listening to music.

Going for a walk or exercising.

Playing with a pet.

Calling a friend.

Keeping a positive internal dialogue ("I made a mistake, but I know how to react next time").

Engaging in mindfulness practices.

Practicing deep breathing.

In addition to aiding in mood improvement, coping skills are an excellent way to practice purposeful behavior. Strong emotions can sometimes cause you to act in a manner that you may regret later. This is especially true for adolescents, who tend to act more reactively and impulsively than adults. Coping skills can help you control your behavior by giving you the space to think before acting.

How do you model the important skills? Here are some tips.

Give Yourself Space When You Need It

One of the surest ways to manage your emotions in a stressful situation is to remove yourself from it, even if only for a moment. Leaving the room before emotions become overwhelming can reduce the likelihood of throwing a fit in front of others while showing them that taking a break from recognizing and dealing with strong emotions is okay.

Walking away from unresolved problems or conflicts can feel uncomfortable and even seem like a way to ignore them. But it's important to remember that emotions tend to build up in intensity until you get some distance from what triggered it.

It's helpful to think about the life cycle of emotions and realize that moving away from those triggers naturally reduces that emotion. That's an important thing to focus on working on; the idea is that you can ask yourself, 'When are my emotions so strong, or what do I need to do to get rid of that?' When you give yourself space, you can think about additional coping skills.

Of course, it's important not to be left unattended; ask for help if you need it in potentially unsafe situations. If you feel overwhelmed or too small to be alone, ensure a trusted adult can be with you.

Talk to Your Parents to Find Out How They Handle Their Emotions

When you want to know more about your emotions, it can be helpful to clarify your intentions by talking and using the coping strategies you already know.

This is especially helpful for you when it becomes more difficult to understand the meaning of certain actions without a verbal explanation. For example, if you need to leave for a few minutes, do so to process the emotions before leaving the room. The plan is to talk to your parents and tell them what you are feeling and ask how they handle it. If the same thing happens to you, ask them if you can talk to a professional to help you overcome the emotions.

You can find several stories that can also be valuable tools for knowing how to deal with emotions because talking about how you feel on an emotional level can give you the opportunity to encourage healthy patterns of behavior without being overwhelmed by feelings.

Be Kind to Yourself

Of course, coping with difficult emotions with intention and grace is easier said than done. So, when you're feeling down, go ahead and be kind to yourself.

I encourage you to start slowly in the process of being kind to yourself. Regularly practicing one or two healthy stress management techniques can serve to reduce conflict and model healthy behavior toward others while increasing your confidence in yourself.

Remember that being kind to yourself is one of the most important coping skills you can count on in this process. Let go of that tendency to be self-critical, and you can quickly adapt to it. One of the most effective ways to deal with negative internal dialogue is to find compassion for yourself (especially!) when you make a mistake. Talking about yourself lovingly and celebrating your accomplishments (even if they seem small) is a crucial way to care for yourself and an essential part of living at home.

Mindfulness

Mindfulness is that path where you are aware of the present; you don't go into the past or the future but enjoy this instant.

What Is Mindfulness?

Is mindfulness meditation? Is it a new relaxation technique? Does it leave your mind blank? These are some of the questions often heard from those who want to use mindfulness to focus.

Mindfulness has burst into our society and can cause confusion and misunderstanding. We can all see how, on certain occasions, it has been labeled as a panacea, and that is not true, although it is good in many ways, especially for you.

The benefits that can bring the practice of mindfulness are enormous, but it depends largely on regularity and continuity, i.e., paying attention to your life consciously.

Worrying, rambling, or recurring thoughts are associated with alterations in neuroendocrine, metabolic, neuromuscular, autoimmune, and cardiovascular processes, so reducing them can positively impact all these domains.

Practicing mindfulness can also help relieve chronic pain, according to research conducted on patients with fibromyalgia and low back pain. On the other hand, practicing mindfulness may reduce the risk of Alzheimer's disease, and a growing body of research is examining its benefits in treating people with dementia or severe mental disorders.

Much is still unknown about the effects of meditation on our brain physiology. Still, there is already evidence that it can activate neural structures associated with attention and help regulate mood.

In short, it improves your quality of life, although it also requires effort and commitment on your part, as changing the inattentive habits you develop year after year is no easy task; if you focus on enjoying the process and learning from it, you will succeed.

Meditation helps you be aware of each experience and accept it instead of making judgments. When you practice it, whether it's 5 or 40 minutes, it's not about avoiding thoughts or getting rid of ideas, it's about sincerely observing and letting go of everything that crosses your mind. It takes a little patience at first and accepting that you may be distracted. You are learning to breathe consciously and observe where your mind is with each breath.

5 Reasons Why You Should Take Up Mindfulness

Here are the reasons why you might want to start doing mindfulness exercises.

Reason 1: It Helps to Manage Stress and Anxiety

The lifestyle in Western society can cause many people to suffer from stress, which leads to mental health problems such as depression or anxiety, especially nowadays. This starts from youth due to the abundant school commitments, sports, girlfriend, rules at home, in short...

In this sense, meditation and mindfulness reduce cortisol levels, a hormone activated in stressful situations. Cortisol is necessary for the body as it regulates and mobilizes energy in these situations, but it can cause side effects if you consume it too much.

Reason 2: It Ends Insomnia Problems

Mindfulness can help you sleep better at night. People who practice it show better control over their emotions and behavior during the day. At night, cortisol levels are lower, which helps them sleep better. If you find it hard to sleep and are glued to your cell phone at night, this will surely help you.

Reason 3: It Protects the Brain

According to a study by Harvard University and Massachusetts General Hospital, mindfulness increases the size of telomeres, structures located at the ends of chromosomes that are directly related to aging and the development of certain related conditions.

The simple fact that you practice it will help protect the brain in the long run.

Reason 4: It Helps You Concentrate

Mindfulness is designed to train awareness and undivided attention to direct these mental processes voluntarily.

According to a Psychology Journal article, mindfulness correlates positively with cognitive flexibility and attention function.

Reason 5: It Develops Emotional Intelligence

Through the practice of mindfulness, self-awareness, and self-knowledge are intensified, and you will be able to evolve inward. Also, by being compassionate with yourself, things will not affect you too much.

Mindfulness Exercises and Practices

Knowing what mindfulness is all about and its benefits for you, let's start with exercises that will work for you.

Mindful Breathing

This exercise can be done sitting or standing wherever you want. If you can meditate in the lotus position, great; if you can't, it doesn't matter.

Either way, all you need to do is sit still and focus on your breath for one minute.

Start by inhaling and exhaling slowly. One breathing cycle could take about 6 seconds.

Breath in through your nose and out through your mouth; let your breath flow smoothly in and out of your body.

Let go of your thoughts. Let go of whatever you have to do later in the day or pending projects that require your attention. Let the thoughts arise and fall away on their own, becoming one with your breath.

Consciously observe your breath, focusing your attention on its path as it enters your body and energizes you.

Then watch with your awareness as it works its way out of your mouth and dissipates its energy into the world.

If you thought you'd never be able to stay willed and focused on the now, guess what? You're already halfway there!

If you enjoy one minute of this relaxing exercise, why not try it for two or three minutes?

Mindful Observation

This exercise is simple but very powerful, as it helps you to detect and appreciate more deeply the seemingly simple elements of your environment.

The exercise is meant to connect you with the beauty of your natural surroundings, something we tend to overlook when we are running or getting on and off the train on our way to school.

Pick a random object in your immediate environment and focus on observing it for a minute or two. This could be a flower, an insect, or even a cloud or the moon.

Do nothing but look at the item you selected. Sit and look for as long as your attention span allows.

Look at the object as if you are seeing it for the first time.

Visually explore every aspect of your process and immerse yourself in its presence.

Allow yourself to connect with the energy and purpose of nature.

Conscious Meditation

This exercise is ideal for developing a greater awareness and appreciation of simple daily tasks and all that is accomplished.

Think about events that happen more than once a day, things you take for granted, like opening a door.

The moment you touch the handle to open the door, stop for a moment and notice where you are, how you are right now, and where the door will take you.

Likewise, the moment you turn on your computer and start working, take a moment to appreciate the hands that hold the process and the brain that helps you understand how to use the computer.

These "touch point" signals are not necessarily physical.

Example: every time you have a negative thought, you can choose to take a moment to stop, label the thought as useless, and let go of the negativity.

Or maybe every time you smell food, take a moment to stop and be thankful that you are lucky enough to have delicious food to share with family and friends.

Instead of automatically piloting your daily activities, choose a touch point that resonates with you today, occasionally pausing to develop a purposeful awareness of what you are doing and the blessings those actions bring to your life.

Conscious Listening

This exercise is designed to allow your ears to listen to sounds without judgment and train your mind not to be swayed by past experiences and preconceived ideas.

Much of what you "feel" is influenced by yesterday's experiences. For example, you may not like some melody because it reminds you of breakups or another time in your life that made you feel something negative.

The idea of this exercise is that you listen to some music from a neutral perspective, with an awareness of the present moment, free of preconceived ideas.

Choose a piece of music you have never heard before. You may have something you've never heard of, or you may choose to change that song until something catches your attention.

Close your eyes and put on your headphones.

Before you start, try not to get hung up on judging the music by genre, title, or artist name. Instead, ignore any decorum and allow yourself to lose yourself neutrally in a sonic journey during the playback of the song.

Allow yourself to explore every aspect of the track. Even if the music is not to your liking at first, let go of your distaste and give your mind permission to step on the floor and dance with the sound waves.

Explore songs by listening to the dynamics of each instrument. Separate each voice in your head and analyze it one by one.

Focus on the voice: its sound, range, and pitch. If there are several voices, separate them as in step 4.

The idea is to listen carefully and participate fully without bias or judgment about genre, artist, lyrics, or instrumentation. Don't think, listen.

After these exercises, you can combine them with conscious breathing, which I will teach you below.

Chapter #3: Breathing Techniques

During meditation, when you are exercising, on walks, sleeping, or all the time, breathing oxygenates the body. Imagine you can calm your worries or stress by simply breathing and controlling how oxygen enters and leaves your body. This is possible, and I will show you in this chapter.

How Breathing Affects Our Emotions

Relearning to breathe is convenient because this action detoxifies the body, oxygenates the cells, undoes your accumulated emotional blocks, deactivates neurons in the brain regions related to stress, contributes to a sense of well-being, and opens a new vision that makes pleasure the pattern of your life.

In many cases, you only use 10% of your breathing capacity when the ideal is to use it 100%, using a technique that I will explain later.

The benefits of retraining your breathing to 100% of your capacity are many, and you will feel them both physically and psychologically. On a physical level, there is the power of breathing to relax internal organs, reduce sensitivity to pain, regulate stress, or eliminate toxins. At the same time, on a psychological level, it helps to expel emotional garbage from the body and improve your inner peace and interpersonal relationships. This can be achieved by regulating the rhythm of breathing.

Recently, it has also been discovered that breathing has a nucleus in the brain called a respiratory pacemaker, a point that activates and deactivates according to the rhythm of breathing.

According to research, every emotion has its breath, and we never breathe in the same way. We breathe according to the emotion we are in at one moment or another, so by changing your breathing, you can change the emotions.

You may have noticed that, for example, when facing negative emotions such as fear or anger, or even in stressful situations, you breathe faster than usual, hindering all the physical and psychological benefits that proper breathing can bring you.

Faster breathing occurs during emotions such as fear or anger. This breathing activates the "breathing pacemaker;" when you want to stop breathing, that point in the brain or pacemaker slows down.

While some people choose three seconds for inhalations and six for exhalations, I propose four (4 seconds) for inhalations and eight for exhalations in this method. In this way, the abdomen and chest breathe completely. Research has found that full breathing is the healthiest, the most natural, and the least tiring, allowing you to use all resources to bring air to the whole body.

The Role of Joy

Joy is the basic emotion you should work on to re-educate your breathing and, ultimately, manage your feelings better. It is the only positive emotion that all humans are born with. In this case, the breathing is completely abdominal, with all your airway. Positive emotions help you move forward, and joy is a restorative, creative, feel-good emotion that drives you to have something.

Psychologists have come up with a slow, deep, full pattern of happy breathing to help you move forward and manage emotions.

Be aware of where you breathe and where you don't. The first reference for a full breath is the abdomen, notice if it moves or not. You have to breathe with your belly, you have to move it, let the air in and out, and your abdomen swell.

Then I recommend you to inhale 4 times (4 seconds per time) and exhale for 8 seconds each time. With this basic abdominal breathing, you activate low reflex breathing, which already lowers the blood pressure because the sympathetic nervous system is disconnected.

Next, I recommend repeating this breathing pattern over the abdomen, counting to 5 seconds as you inhale and 10 seconds as you exhale. Do this gradually until you inhale across the chest, then into the collarbone area.

Repeat this pattern in such a way that you can inhale in 8 seconds and exhale in 16 seconds. All this leads to the fact that you can manage emotions by breathing.

This technique of transforming negative emotions into positive ones has been registered as Integrated Transformational Breathing, which is known to be a method to oxygenate the body's systems and help you achieve peace of mind anytime, anywhere; ultimately, it will help you manage emotions and make you happier.

Breathing Exercises for Different Emotions

These are some breathing exercises that will help you work on various emotions.

Anger

The easiest of the exercises is presented here. It is used in stressful or difficult situations. The idea is to inhale air through the nose, hold it in the lungs and finally expel it gently through the mouth. Each step should last about four seconds.

4-7-8 Breathing Technique

This is one of my favorites for its simplicity and effectiveness. Get into a comfortable position (you can be sitting or lying down) before you begin. To use the 4-7-8 technique, focus on the following breathing patterns:

Empty the lungs of oxygen.

Inhale quietly through your nose for 4 seconds.

Hold your breath for 7 seconds.

Release forcefully through your mouth, pursing your lips, and making a "whistling" sound for 8 seconds.

Repeat this cycle four times, or do it for a minute or two.

Anxiety

In this case, the breathing will be abdominal. To do this, you need a comfortable place, preferably sitting or lying down.

First, inhale through your nose for about four seconds, allowing the air to stay in your body for a while, then exhale gently through your mouth.

Take a long inhalation to let a lot of air into your body.

By placing one hand on your abdomen and the other on your chest, you can check that the air is being sent correctly to the intended area.

The hand on the chest should not move as you inhale, and at the same time, you should feel the air filling your belly.

Equal Breathing Exercises

This simple exercise is one of the most effective in reducing anxiety. It involves you breathing at a "regular" rate of 4 seconds:

Take in air through your nose for 4 seconds and then release through your mouth for another 4 seconds. Repeat this cycle at least three times, but you can repeat as many times as you like. Over time, you are likely to hold your breath twice as long as those who practice disciplines that involve breath control, such as yoga or meditation.

If this is your first experience with this practice, you may want to listen to some guided meditation, which has tips on how to position yourself and breathe for meditation.

Uncontrolled Crying

This is an exercise to stop crying through breathing:

Focus on your breathing. Crying is a response to heightened emotions, and the relaxing effect of the breath can help you suppress the crying.

Maybe you just remembered something sad, broke up with your boyfriend, or something tragic happened in your life. Calming down is an important part of avoiding tears. Also, focusing on your breathing as you do in meditation can help you control your emotions and restore inner peace.

When you feel tears welling up in your eyes, take a deep breath in through your nose and exhale slowly through your mouth. Doing this will loosen the lump that forms in your throat when you are on the verge of tears and stabilizes your thoughts and emotions.

Try counting to 10. Inhale through your nose as you count and exhale through your mouth between counts. Counting will help you focus on your breathing instead of thinking you will cry.

When you are faced with something that makes you cry, even a deep breath can calm you down. Take a deep breath in, hold it for a moment, and then exhale. At that moment, just focus on the air going in and out of your lungs. Breathing deeply will also give you a moment of pause before you face the cause of your pain.

Move your eyes to control the tears. If you're in situations that make you tearful but don't want to express your emotions to others, moving your eyes can help you control your tears. Research suggests that several blinks help stop the flow of tears.

Blink a couple of times, wipe tears from the corners of your eyes, or squint and roll your eyes rapidly. Of course, you probably only want to do this if you know no one is looking at you, since in addition to being mentally distracted by having to squint, it will also physically prevent tears from forming.

Close your eyes. Closing your eyes will give you time to process whatever is going on. Also, closing your eyes and taking deep breaths will help you calm down and focus on not crying.

Distract yourself with body movements. When you're on the verge of tears, focusing on other things is good. Distracting yourself is one way to avoid crying.

Compress your upper thighs or clasp your hands together and squeeze them. The stress of this action should be enough to distract you from the urge to cry.

Find something else to squeeze, whether it's an anti-stress toy, a pillow, part of a shirt, or a loved one's hand.

Press your tongue against the roof of your mouth or your teeth.

Relax your facial expressions. Frowning can make you cry more easily because our facial expressions affect our emotions. To help you avoid crying, try to maintain a neutral facial expression in any situation where you feel you are about to cry. Relax the muscles around your forehead and mouth and avoid a worried or distressed expression.

If appropriate or feasible, step away for a few minutes and try smiling to avoid crying. Some research shows that smiling can positively change your mood, even when you don't feel like smiling.

Loosen the lump in your throat. One of the hardest parts of trying to hold back tears is getting rid of the lump in your throat that forms when something makes you want to cry. When your body senses that you are under stress, one of the responses of the autonomic nervous system is to open the glottis, the muscle that controls the opening of the larynx at the back of the throat. If the glottis is open, we feel a lump in our throat when we try to swallow.

Drink a glass of water to release the pressure causing the glottis to open. Drinking water will relax the throat muscles and calm the nerves.

If you don't have water at hand, breathe calmly and swallow slowly several times. Breathing will help you calm down and several swallows will tell your body that it doesn't need to keep the glottis open.

Yawning. Yawning helps relax the throat muscles, which means it relieves tension when the glottis opens.

Think of other things you can concentrate on. Sometimes you can hold back tears by turning your attention to other things. For example, you can change your focus by mentally solving some simple math problems. Adding decimals mentally or going over multiplication tables can distract you from the events that make you feel bad and help you calm down.

Try thinking of the words to a favorite song. Memorizing the words and singing the tune in your head will distract you from whatever is bothering you. Try imagining the words to a happy or funny song to lift your spirits.

Think of something fun. When you're faced with something that makes you want to cry, it may seem like you have a hard time holding it in, but thinking of something funny can help you hold back the tears. Think of episodes from your past that made you laugh, such as memories, movie scenes, or jokes you heard.

Remind yourself you are a strong person. When you are about to cry, giving yourself a mental boost can help you overcome the urge to cry. Explain to yourself that feeling sad is okay, but now is not the time to show it. Remind yourself of the reasons you couldn't cry at that moment, such as you don't want to cry in front of people you don't know; you want to be strong to support someone, etc. Promise yourself that even if you have to hold back at that moment, you can vent your sadness later.

Stress

This technique, widely used in the world of yoga, is based on alternating between the nostrils during inspiration. First, cover one nostril and inhale deeply through the free nostril. After inhaling, proceed to cover the nostril through which the air enters and uncover the other nostril through which the exhalation will occur.

Incorporate Breathing into Your Daily Routine

Incorporating conscious breathing into your daily life is simple and easy for everyone. Here are some tips for you to add mindful breathing exercises into your daily life:

Find a Quiet, Comfortable Place

Finding a quiet, peaceful space is essential to practice mindful breathing. You can sit in a comfortable chair or on the floor, or even do it standing up. You must feel comfortable and must maintain your posture during meditation.

Establish a Regular Schedule

Establishing a routine is essential to include mindful breathing in your life. You can do it at any time of the day, but I advise doing it at the same time every day. For example, you can do it at the beginning of the day, during lunchtime, or before bedtime.

Start With Short Sessions

Start with short bursts of conscious breathing for 3 to 5 minutes. You can increase the length of a session over time. What matters is that it is something you can maintain regularly.

How to Use a Guide or App

Use one of the apps that offer guided meditation and mindful breathing techniques. These can be especially helpful if you are new to the practice or if you have trouble concentrating during meditation.

In addition, some apps allow you to customize your meditation experience by choosing the length of the meditation, the narrator's voice, and background music.

Progressive Muscle Relaxation

One of the most widely used relaxation procedures is the classic progressive muscle relaxation technique, developed in 1938 by the American physician Edmund Jacobson. A common practice is to start with progressive muscle relaxation and end with some relaxation strategies. Visualization helps to maximize mental relaxation.

Progressive muscle relaxation is based on identifying which muscles are tense or overactive and acting on them to relax them. It is called progressive because the different muscle groups relax gradually, even if you initially do not realize how much tension they have accumulated.

The original program consisted of more than 60 exercises, but now there are shorter programs based on his technique.

Proper training and the habit of performing these exercises can facilitate the "disguised" practice of them, allowing relaxation in everyday situations where it is not possible to be alone or assume comfortable positions.

Phases of Jacobson's Relaxation

There are three phases in this method, during which it is important to use the diaphragmatic breathing technique, inhaling slowly, bringing the air to the belly, and exhaling slowly.

You should start with a comfortable and correct posture, such as sitting in a chair with a straight back, shoulders relaxed, and avoiding a tense neck position, which should align the spine with the head.

It is helpful to imagine a string over your head, pulling you gently so that you do not fall forward, backward, or sideways. Ensure you do not cross your legs and that your feet are firmly planted on the floor. Performing these exercises should not cause any pain or discomfort. If it does, you should discontinue the practice and consult a physician if the problem persists.

Why Progressive Muscle Relaxation Will Help You Self-Regulate

The scientific explanation behind the effectiveness of Jacobson's relaxation is that it directly affects the autonomic nervous system (ANS). This part of the body is responsible for controlling involuntary actions such as breathing, blood vessel dilation, heart rate, sweating, salivation, and digestion.

The ANS is divided into parasympathetic and sympathetic branches. The sympathetic is the branch that prepares the body for action; the parasympathetic is the branch that prepares the body for rest.

The relaxing effect of Jacobson's progressive relaxation technique lies in its ability to stimulate the parasympathetic branch and reduce the physiological effects of the sympathetic branch, which is activated in situations of stress and anxiety.

Progressive Muscle Relaxation Exercise

Let's start with the exercises step by step through their phases:

First Phase: Tension-Relaxation

This involves tensing and relaxing different muscles while maintaining the position for about 10-15 seconds. In this example we will focus on four muscle groups:

Face

Forehead: frown tightly and then slowly relax it.

Eyes: close and squeeze, feeling the tension in the eyelids, and then loosen them.

Lips and jaw: tighten lips and teeth and then relax; leaving the mouth ajar, separate the teeth, and leave the tongue loose.

Neck and Shoulders

Neck: Lower your head toward your chest, and feel the tension in the back of your neck. Relax the muscles and return the head to the starting position, in alignment with the spine.

Shoulders: Slowly tilt the shoulders forward with the back forward, bringing the elbows back; feel the tension in the back. Remove the tension by bringing the back to the original position and letting the arms rest on the legs.

Arms and hands: rest your arms on your legs, clench your fists, and feel the tension in your arms, forearms, and hands. To release tension, unclench your fists and rest your fingers on your legs.

Abdomen

The abdominal muscles can be tightened by "tucking in your belly" and then relaxing.

Legs

Stretch one leg by raising your foot and toes. As you extend them back, feel the tension in the entire leg: hip, knee, thigh, calf, and foot.

Now slowly relax, turn your toes forward, and lower your leg until the soles of your feet touch the floor. Do the same with the other leg.

Second Phase: Mental Review

This involves mentally examining all the muscle groups to see if they are relaxed, or if they need to be further relaxed.

Third Phase: Mental Relaxation

The third stage consists of focusing your attention on a state of calm. It may be helpful to imagine a pleasant scene that evokes different emotions. A good example is to imagine yourself lying on the beach; evoke the colors, the sound of the waves, the feel of the sand, the smell of the sea, the warmth of the sun, the breeze on your skin, etc...

Chapter #4: Every Problem Is a Situation to Solve

As I have already told you in other chapters, problems will always appear in our lives; we cannot avoid them, so we must learn to analyze, fragment, and face them. In this chapter, I want to teach you how to identify them, find solutions with different tools, touch the ground when they overwhelm you, and evaluate the best solution.

Identifying Problems and Challenges

One of the main tasks in everyday life is problem-solving. How many times have you heard the phrase "I have a problem?" A problem can be defined as an unfavorable contradiction between "what is" and "what should be." Problems are often conflicts that require a solution, even if it is not always obvious.

There are many classifications of problems, for example, by the number of possible solutions you can find:

A convergent problem is a problem that has a unique solution or a defined set of solutions. Some convergent problems are: Answering a topic from memory, solving a mathematical problem, summarizing, reasoning, finding a definition in a dictionary, etc.

Divergent questions, on the other hand, are those that have an uncertain number of possible answers and depend on human creativity, for example: To announce a school event, how to get 1,000 euros in one week, how to fix a broken item, etc.

Whatever our problems are, the difficulty is in dealing with them. Many people get stuck when they encounter a problem, do not know how to deal with it or do not find an acceptable solution, or do not respond adequately when faced with any difficulty...

To optimally resolve the situations that manifest themselves, you must first identify and analyze the relevant problems.

Some questions that can help you identify them may be: What is the source of the problem? Where does the issue come from? What perspectives were considered? What kind of reasoning arises? Is it really my problem?

Here are some steps to help you identify a problem:

Step 1: Situation symptom analysis: You recognize that things are not going well or that you are not achieving the desired result. If you don't change the current situation, you may see threats in the future. Sometimes, what you miss today may be your problem tomorrow.

Step 2: Detect the cause of the problem: This step consists of detecting the symptoms of the problem situation that lead you to the cause of the problem. Sometimes, what you see with the naked eye is just the tip of the iceberg. The 5 whys technique (described later) can help you accomplish this task.

Step 3: Prioritize: Once you have found and identified the problems, you must rank them in order of importance to solve them in batches. If you start with all of them at once, you run the risk of not being able to solve any of them. To rank them correctly, consider the timelines and the impact each of them may have.

Step 4: Write the problem: The problem statement should be concise and specific, and should point out the deviation to be addressed, i.e., the deviation that exists between the desired situation and the current circumstances. "The words you use to define a problem in some way guide the direction of the solution."

In addition to all the keys I've laid out for you, give yourself time to identify the problem and be prepared so that your fears or blocks don't paralyze you or cause you to stop being objective, thus preventing you from coming up with the best solution.

Brainstorming Solutions

It is often said that inspiration comes when you least expect it, but this is an ineffective way to foster innovation and creativity. Think of a time when you or a group you were in had to solve a particular problem. It could be as simple as deciding on a theme for a school party or identifying a strategy to achieve the best test score for the current term. Once you start thinking of ideas, your mind goes blank.

What you need are strategies to help you unleash your creativity. Brainstorming is the answer. Integrating brainstorming as part of the problem-solving process fosters collaboration and innovative thinking and can lead to the best ideas. Practice the following steps to learn how to generate them like a pro.

What Is Brainstorming and What Is It for?

As the name suggests, brainstorming is about getting brains flowing to solve problems through a series of creative solutions. It is a technique to generate ideas and stimulate creativity.

Typically, people brainstorm ideas at the beginning of a project to find innovative solutions to current problems, but this technique can also be applied when new concepts are needed.

While brainstorming is often used in groups, it can also be a great tool for people working on personal goals and projects, such as deciding what to write about or what new craft project to start.

Brainstorming makes it easy for you to do the following:

Consider all possibilities.

Avoid creative burnout.

Encourage collaboration.

Encourage creativity and innovation.

Generate several ideas in a short time.

Gather other perspectives.

The golden rule of brainstorming sessions is "quantity over quality." The more notions you have, the greater the chances of succeeding. So, especially during brainstorming alone or in a group, you must make sure that criticism is put aside and that it is understood that there are no bad ideas, only good ones.

Of course, not all brainstorming sessions are perfect. Here are some common challenges you may face when organizing a brainstorming session:

Unbalanced conversations, as sometimes extroverts take the lead in discussions.

Nothing new arises. The anchoring effect occurs when brainstorming sticks to some original ideas that have already been shared and members don't come up with new ones.

Awkward silence, which always occurs when participants are not ready.

You've probably been through a few of these awkward brainstorming sessions. Fortunately, there is plenty of trial and error and unconventional brainstorming techniques or tools to address these problems.

Starbursting

This is a visual trick for brainstorming. The starbursting technique should be used once ideas have been focused on specific concepts. To start such a session, write an idea in the center of the whiteboard and draw a six-pointed star around it. There will be a problem at each end:

How?

When?

Where?

Why?

What?

Who?

Analyze each question and how it relates to your thoughts. For example, "Who will want to go to the beach at the end of the school year?" or "When should we have the program ready?" will help you explore possible scenarios or uncover potential obstacles you hadn't considered before.

The Five "Whys?"

Like the starburst technique, the "why" practice helps you assess the strength of your brainstorming. Challenge yourself to ask yourself the why and how of a problem or idea at least five times, analyze the problems that arise, and most importantly, think about how to solve them. To better organize your thoughts, consider using a flow chart or fishtail diagram you find useful with this technique.

Ideal for: Individual or group brainstorming and in-depth analysis of ideas.

SWOT Analysis

You are probably already familiar with SWOT analysis because it is associated with strategic planning, and you must have been taught it in school. You may be surprised to learn that this concept can also be used as a brainstorming exercise to validate specific notions. Discuss the following aspects of the topic to determine if it is worth implementing:

Strengths: how does the idea stand out, or what benefits does it offer over others?

Weaknesses: Are there any flaws in the idea that could compromise implementation?

Opportunities: What can you capitalize on based on this idea?

Threats: What problems can occur when this idea is implemented?

Suitable for: individual or group brainstorming and in-depth idea analysis.

The "How Now Wow" Matrix

The "How Now Wow" brainstorming technique is about categorizing brainstorming ideas according to originality and ease of use. Once several ideas are gathered, either individually or in a team, they are analyzed to see how they fall within the spectrum of this technique.

"How" ideas (how to put them into practice) are original ideas but cannot be implemented.

"Now" ideas are not realistic but are easy to implement in practice at the moment.

"Wow" (surprise) ideas are those that have never been thought of and are also easy to implement.

Of course, it is convenient to have as many "wow" ideas as possible, both because they can be put into practice and because they can differentiate you from others and break the monotony of life. To better organize your thoughts, consider using a four-square matrix with difficulty weights on the Y-axis, and innovation weights on the X-axis.

Ideal for: Individuals or groups brainstorming and looking for actionable solutions.

Factor Analysis

As the name suggests, factor analysis is a brainstorming technique to analyze the factors or "causes" of a problem. To use this brainstorming technique, you simply ask yourself, "What caused [insert question]?" Then, "What caused [insert answer to the previous question]?" It is similar to the "why" analysis. The deeper you study a problem, the better you can analyze it, and the more confidence you will have to implement the best solution to those problems.

Ideal for: individual or group brainstorming and in-depth analysis of ideas.

Mind Mapping

Another visual brainstorming technique focuses on mind maps with anchoring effects, a very common challenge in which brainstorming participants start with fixed initial ideas rather than generating new ones. Mind maps are used with initial notions to generate subsequent ideas.

To make them, you will need a large sheet of paper or a whiteboard. Start by writing about the topic, then draw lines that connect to other related ideas. Their main contribution is that they help you understand the problem at hand and the factors that can affect or even accelerate implementation.

Best for: Individual or group brainstorming and those who are more adept at visual thinking.

Gap Analysis

When you have doubts about how to make an idea a reality, that's when the opportunity to "close the gap"—to deal with the obstacles that stand in the way—comes into play. Start by stating where you are now and move toward where you want to be.

It's worth writing it down on a large sheet of paper or whiteboard for all brainstormers to see, or if this is just for you, it's also helpful with a flow chart or mind map attached. After you have captured it on the sheet, list the obstacles that prevent you from reaching your destination and develop a solution for each obstacle. At the end of your brainstorming sessions, a clear plan should emerge on how to get where you want to go.

Best for: Individual or team brainstorming, and especially for those who are better at visuals and those who refine workable solutions.

Grounding Techniques That Will Help You Calm Down and Be Present

All living beings that inhabit the earth are connected to each other and the earth. However, in the constant transformation of their evolution and their way of life, Man is moving further and further away from this connection, even from himself and his present.

Re-establishing this connection is a practice that can help you to stop living in the past with unwanted memories and free yourself from negative emotions. In addition, it is a way to reconnect with your true essence and focus on what is happening at the moment.

You can use grounding techniques in almost any situation to reduce painful emotions, such as:

Anxiety

Dissociation

Self-injurious urges

Traumatic memories

Post-traumatic stress disorder

Substance use disorder

Physical Techniques to Connect with Your Senses

Consider these techniques:

Put Your Hands in Water

Pay attention to the temperature of the water and how it feels on the fingertips, palms, and backs of your hands.

Do all parts of the hand feel the same? You can use different water temperatures to experience the diverse sensations on your skin and learn how each situation feels.

Another option is to take an ice cube—how does it feel to hold it in your hand? How long does it take to start melting, and how does it feel when it melts? Notice how that nagging thought recedes.

Take Objects Around You

Feel everything you touch, paying attention to its color, shape, texture, weight, and how it feels when you touch it and hold it. What is its texture: soft, firm, or pleasant to the touch? Is it heavy or light? Is it warm or cold?

Take a Deep Breath and Enjoy a Scent

First, inhale and exhale slowly. Repeat several times, feel the breath filling your lungs, and notice how it feels when you breathe it out.

Then choose your favorite scent. It can be a cup of tea, an herb or spice, an essential oil, your favorite soap, or a scented candle. Inhale a scent slowly and deeply, and try to notice its qualities: sweet, spicy, sour, citrus, floral, etc., and notice the reaction it provokes in you.

Taste a Food or Drink

Choose what you like the most, but don't get carried away by emotions, don't eat it; enjoy it little by little. Take a small bite or a sip and take the time to fully taste the texture, the flavor, and the sensation it leaves in your mouth. Think about how it tastes and smells, and identify the different flavors that linger on your tongue.

Listen to Your Surroundings

Take a few minutes to listen to the noises and sounds around you. Do you hear birds singing, dogs barking, or people whispering? Can you hear the noise of equipment such as cars, motorcycles, or your neighbor's lawnmower? Can you hear music from your car, home, or office? Let the sound invade you and remind you where you are.

Evaluate and Select the Best Solution

Here are the steps to work through the problem:

Identifying the Problem

You have to find the problem that affects the goals you want to pursue, the problem may be current, or it may be the cause of many conflicts in the environment. To locate the problem, you can ask yourself the following questions: Where is it happening? What happened? When did it happen? Who is involved? Why is this problem happening?

Analyzing the Problem

To do an analysis, you must have all the data and information and have confidence in that data. Once you have all that information, you must understand the problem, and this will happen as you seek to define it, build it and analyze its flaws. If the problem is complex, you should break it down into several parts so that each one can describe the specific problem.

Generate Potential Solutions to the Problem

To solve a problem, multiple alternatives can be generated, which are based on uncertainty. To find these solutions, you must state the desired conditions in the first two steps of your plan.

Decision-Making and Action Plans

These are the fundamentals for you to make a decision:

Define the problems

Collect data

Generate options

Choose a course of action

To make decisions, you must analyze the different aspects, how you approach these decisions based on the problem to be solved, the possible solutions, and the degree of risk, each aspect will assume.

To close this chapter, simply put, what you have to do to solve this problem is to analyze each possible solution, if your decision will generate problems or not, if you are acting well or not, and choose the options that leave the least bad consequences, or take the most painful decision, even though it may not be the best one.

Chapter #5: Communication Superpowers

Surely you have been told at school that all living beings communicate between themselves and that this is elementary to relate to each other. I want you to see it with greater importance than you have seen it so far, increasing communication so that you know how to get the most out of it by talking to others, that you assume it as a fundamental pillar to communicate with people from any space, take action for active listening and know how to speak assertively with others.

Effective Communication Is the Key

Language and the ability to connect and share knowledge are fundamental aspects of coexistence and even human beings' physical and mental health.

Communication is fundamental, as it allows you to interact with your fellow human beings and also with other animal species. In your daily life, you should not fail to do this because all movement, or even the absence of it, is communication.

But it is worth asking, are we capable of communicating effectively?

Knowing How to Express Yourself and Make Yourself Understood

Communication involves the exchange of information between two or more subjects using various codes they can transmit.

But doing this efficiently doesn't just mean that subject A sends messages to subject B. To communicate effectively, it is necessary to create an atmosphere of mutual understanding and respect in which the interlocutors have messages that are conveyed effectively, clearly, concisely, and consistently with the content of the message and the attitude in communication.

Crucially, the act allows both components to express themselves and be actively heard, maintaining a language appropriate to the abilities of both subjects.

We are immersed in an increasingly individualistic society, which hinders effective communication. People tend to express themselves constantly without leaving space for the other person to respond, without listening to what the other person has to say, in addition to often using contradictions and ambiguities that can lead to different interpretations.

Keys to Effective Communication

Below, you will find a series of aspects to remember for effective communication.

Maintain Eye Contact

Appearance is an essential element of communicative behavior because it is highly expressive. Naturally holding your gaze is a sign of interest in what your interlocutors are telling you. As part of the communicative act, listeners are more likely to feel cared for and accepted. Eyes that avoid eye contact can send the message of a lack of interest, confidence, or even a lie in the act of communication.

Use an Appropriate Tone of Voice for the Context

Intonation is also an important factor in effective communication. The right tone depends on the type of communication you are working on, the content of the message, or the circumstances in which it occurs. In general, I recommend a tone without deep ups and downs.

Let Your Body Support Your Message

There is much more to gestural and postural communication than most people realize. Depending on your nonverbal language, you can support or even refute the verbal information, giving different interpretations. Posture and gestures should accompany the message being conveyed, even enrich it.

Practice Active Listening

A common mistake many people make today is that they tend to talk but do not listen to what the other person says as if the other person's reaction is unimportant. With this, the other person feels neglected, and, in turn, the interest in maintaining the communicative behavior ceases.

Respect the Other's Opinion

You can have very specific positions on a particular issue, but this does not have to coincide with that of others. If you want to communicate effectively, you must be able to unconditionally accept the possibility of finding different positions and respect them, even if you disagree with them, however distant they may be from your position.

Use a Clear Message

It is important that messages are concise and that you use understandable and not vague vocabulary. Otherwise, you may generate multiple interpretations, thus hindering the purposes for which you want to communicate.

Use Language Adjusted to the Interlocutor's Reality

If you want to communicate effectively, you must consider that not all audiences have the same level of education, knowledge, vocabulary, or even understanding. It is necessary to adapt the type of language used to the real situation of the public you are addressing. You don't speak the same way to your classmates as you do to a first grader.

Practice Empathy

Connecting and building a positive relationship with your interlocutors is essential if you want to create an environment conducive to mutual understanding and smooth communication.

Don't Use Rigid Messages

When communicating, it is easy to use stereotypes and familiar formulas. While formalism may be necessary in some cases, the use of standardized messages often provides a cold, impersonal perspective on communication that reduces genuine interest and leads listeners to wonder what the message's sender is doing.

You should also keep in mind that while it is good to plan for possible questions, you need to give your speech a certain spontaneity that makes it seem real.

Keep the Context in Mind

Going to a meeting, going to a wedding, or going to a funeral is not the same thing. The message must be adapted to the subject and its important reality and consider the context in which the communication takes place.

Act With Determination

In communication, try not to overwhelm the other party, impose your will without listening to the other party's opinions, or let yourself be dragged along by the other party. You must defend your positions with full respect for the opinions of your interlocutor.

Be Consistent

If you want your communication to be effective, it is useful to focus on what the other person can understand without having to over-interpret and that the meaning of the message does not change from one moment to the next. Continuity of discourse is essential.

Use Questions and Interpretations

What your interlocutor thinks you are interested in is an important aspect of effective communication. Just asking questions shows that you are listening and allows you to finish understanding or to make the other person understand parts of the message that are not clear. Paraphrasing helps you show that you are listening while allowing you to organize the essential parts of the speech.

Respect Turns

Communicative behavior is established between two or more people. If we are talking about verbal communication, everyone involved must be committed to respecting the other's right to speak rather than constantly interrupting their interlocutor's messages.

Anticipate Possible Responses

Doubts and questions often arise from the person receiving the information, or different events may occur during the communication. Anticipating this possibility and having a plan of action or possible response ready will help make the message safer and more effective.

Don't Just Call the Shots

Effective communication begins with respect and education of the person communicating. If messages are sent in an authoritarian manner, they can be seen as punitive, generating rejection and resistance.

Manage Your Emotions

Different feelings, moods, and emotions often arise during communication. While they can be exposed and even increase efficiency by improving understanding between interlocutors, you should not let them go to extremes that prevent you from exchanging information or hinder the achievement of your communication objectives.

Have a Goal and Be Honest About It

If you intend to communicate effectively, you must be clear about your goal and be able to discuss and argue in such a way that communication can facilitate its realization. It is highly recommended to be honest and real and not try to manipulate the other person.

Discuss Topics One by One

Starting with one topic, switching to other topics, and returning to the original topic can sometimes be effective. Still, if it is not very planned, it can often confuse the audience about what topic is being discussed. To maintain the internal coherence of the speech, it will be helpful to approach topics sequentially.

Avoid Generalizations and Deviations

Clear and concise information is quicker and more effective than going a long way around a topic before reaching the actual goal.

Try to Express Yourself in a Positive Way

Regardless of the type of information conveyed, detailed communications and concepts that are presented from a positive and constructive perspective tend to be more effective and receptive.

Don't Overextend Communication Time

While it may be tempting to give a long, detailed speech to convey many ideas, you must keep in mind that people have a certain attention span, and the longer the discussion, the greater the chances that the information will be conveyed. You can lose it because of the way you deliver it. Short speeches that clarify the different key points are usually more effective. It's like when you present in class, no one pays much attention to you, and if you go on too long, you bore even the teacher.

Maintain Motivation

Keeping people motivated is essential to maintain interest in the exchange and generate some kind of positive outcome. Providing space for your interlocutor to express their doubts, agree with their expressions, and respond to them can be very motivating, as well as attention to the information.

Integrate and Be Open to Adding or Considering Other People's Perspectives

Considering other people's perspectives is important, no matter how hard you try to defend an idea. To make your presentation more effective, it is recommended to use some elements added by others and discuss them spontaneously.

This allows you, on the one hand, to check that the contributions of others have been taken into account, while, on the other hand, you can reinforce or qualify the information to be conveyed.

The Secret of Active Listening

Active listening is a communication strategy that consists of fully listening to a speaker's message to cognitively and empathetically understand what they are saying.

You should consider the following tips and suggestions to do effective active listening. This is something you should always avoid.

Interruptions

You have to wait for the other person to finish. If the other person needs to express what happened to them, you should avoid telling "your story" without letting them finish.

Distractions

When you communicate, your attention is reduced to the "heart" of the conversation, which is usually at the beginning and end of the interchange. Therefore, you should strive to maintain the same level of attention in different parts of the conversation.

Expressions

For example, "Relax, I'm sure nothing's wrong."

Being a "Psychologist Around the House"

Avoid offering solutions and answers to the other person by addressing everything that happened to you without listening to the whole conversation.

Judging

If someone is judged for what they say, they are usually moving away from learning patterns that allow them to tolerate the opinions of others. So you must accept what they tell you, even if you disagree. Build tolerance, self-confidence and even learn to admit mistakes instead of getting frustrated.

Reproach Everything They Say to You

It's best not to reproach others for saying things you don't like, or lecture to correct the way others think. This kind of attitude only alienates you from others.

Versions of a Story

One person is in charge of telling the story. However, before doing so, that person will say that X words are going to be scored for the number of times it appears in the story. When it is finished, the result is asked for, but in return: the scene heard is to be described, and vice versa. Point out how simple it is to selectively show and forget the rest of the story.

The Role of the Blind Man

You can experience this with other people, forming two teams, for example, with classmates from your school. Each team chooses one member to play the role of blindfolded. The plan is that others can help him or her move around the room from one end to the other without bumping into obstacles along the way. You will have an idea of how blind people understand and follow the instructions of others.

The Importance of Assertiveness

Assertiveness is the ability to express your desires, beliefs, feelings, emotions, opinions, tastes, preferences, and opinions in a non-aggressive but socially acceptable manner.

Self-confidence allows you to exercise your right to be an active participant in situations, thus serving as an effective communication tool that facilitates the expression of emotions and thoughts. The goal is not to hurt others but to stand up for yourself and assert yourself, to set a precedent for disagreement, and to try to change behaviors that violate your rights.

What does it mean to be assertive? To answer this question, it is necessary to understand what characterizes a confident person. Some of these are as follows:

They speak with authority. People who speak with authority will not be afraid, will not have expectations, and will not be influenced by what others think of their words. When they speak with authority, they do so out of self-respect, so they earn the respect of others.

They express their emotions. They are the ones who can express their emotions, whether positive or negative. They treat others and themselves with respect. In this way, they can point out what is bothering them without attacking others and looking for a solution to the problem at hand.

They focus on the positive. They can recognize positive aspects of themselves and others.

They take responsibility. They can take responsibility for their actions, and instead of focusing on catastrophic thinking, they look for solutions.

They have great emotional regulation skills. Emotional management is fundamental to good self-confidence. Emotional intelligence and self-confidence go hand in hand.

Below, you'll find a collection of effective assertiveness tips you can start using today.

Fog Bank

Assertiveness fog is all about using strategic phrases to distract attention, and instead of giving in to your initial thoughts, acknowledging other people's arguments and ideas, even if they are complaints. In this way, the position does not count as a direct attack.

It is a manner of regulating negative thoughts and impulsive attitudes. You can stop and look at the situation from a different perspective. In this way, messages can be managed in the most pleasant way.

It is a technique that can be used to:

Saying no decisively.

Avoid criticism when they seek to manipulate you.

Take a stand and not hurt others.

To apply this technique, you must partially agree, but at the same time maintain integrity and make your point clear, and not get carried away by strong emotions. Have the conversation in a firm but calm tone. In environments where you must behave seriously, this technique can be effective when asking questions that may be somewhat difficult to answer.

Assertive Postponement

This assertive technique is about letting the other person realize that it is not the right time to have a heated conversation. The goal is to stop talking to prevent strong emotions from boiling over.

This technique is especially used when the other person does not understand the message you are giving them or their communication starts to become aggressive. It is necessary to convey confident deferrals with empathy, respect, and a calm tone.

Broken Record Technique

The broken record technique is used to make the other party realize that they will not achieve their goals and that you will not be manipulated. It involves repeating an argument consistently with a "no" that supports your point of view.

It can be when you are approached for favors, invitations, or offers that do not interest you. When the other party tries to change your mind, you must stick to your decision and keep repeating the "no" argument over and over again.

I-messaging

"I" messaging involves sending messages such as "I want," "I need," or "I feel" to another person before a conversation. That way, you avoid doing what others ask you to do when you don't want to. Communicate with confidence without worrying about arguments or others imposing their ideas. With this type of information, you help others to put themselves in your place and thus better understand your point of view.

Sandwich Technique

This is another assertive skill needed to express your own opinion without being rude to the other person. It involves saying nice things about the other person first, then saying things you don't like, and finally saying something positive. This is ideal when you want to be critical but express the positive aspects of the other person. It's not making anything up; it's just authentically highlighting the positive.

These assertive communication skills are great for any time and context.

Chapter #6: The Importance of Having a Clearly Defined Goal

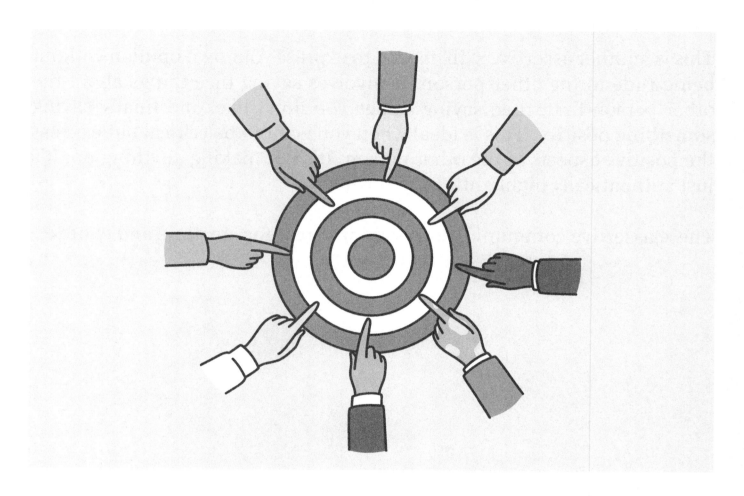

Along the way, you will be able to get on track to achieve the goals you set for yourself by controlling your emotions well, focusing on communicating messages clearly, and defining everything you may be working on. In this chapter, I want to teach you about SMART goals, the steps to manage them, how to track your progress to achieve them, and most importantly, how to work on resilience to deal with those moments when you find it difficult to control certain emotions or when things go wrong.

Set SMART Goals

Thinking about and defining goals is an important part of working on anything you do. Let's talk about it in this section, getting to know what SMART goals are and getting some examples to get you started on them.

One of the keys to being productive at school, at home, or wherever you need to be is knowing how to set goals properly.

We all want to grow to do better things, get good results in school, courses, or wherever, and build better relationships with the people we interact with. You can always pursue these goals, but only if you sit down and think intelligently about how to achieve them.

In other words, "wanting to grow" is not the same as setting out to increase your exam grades by 25% in a year through a series of studies. The former is an aspiration, and the latter is a goal based on specific data, which is achievable, measurable, and reviewable over time. In other words, a SMART objective.

SMART objectives are specific, measurable, achievable, relevant, and timely. They are specific goals that allow you to analyze the performance of your efforts, whether in school or in any area of life, whose work needs to be systematically ordered and measured.

SMART is an acronym that refers to all the characteristics that a good goal should have. Therefore, SMART objectives are:

Specific

Measurable

Achievable

Relevant

Timely

I want you to look at each of these characteristics separately.

SMART objectives are the way to go when you want to set goals. Almost all related things use this famous tool.

If there's one tool that teens can understand, it's this one—you may become familiar with it later! SMART is an acronym that can be used to easily plan and evaluate goals to see if they are effective.

The criteria for SMART goals are based on Locke and Latham's theory, but are easier for anyone, anywhere to implement. When developing SMART objectives, keep the following points in mind. Here are some examples:

The SMART Objective: S—Specific

Being specific means that objectives must be formulated precisely. What do you really need to change? Avoid ambiguous statements or overly broad and complex descriptions to make sure you start working in the right direction from the beginning. At best, a precise sentence is sufficient for the purposes of the SMART method.

A practical example of a specific goal:

Increase guitar playing ability to achieve an entire song. This objective is specific because it consists of a clear and defined goal.

The SMART Objective: M—Measurable

The objectives to be achieved must be measurable and evaluable. Only then can it be determined whether the objectives have been accomplished. For this purpose, KPIs (Key Performance Indicators) are of great importance.

A practical example of a measurable objective:

Certain objectives are easier to define than others; for example, if you are a swimmer and want to reduce the 100-meter freestyle swim by 5 seconds. This way, you can make a simple comparison between where you are and your goal, so it will be easy for you to determine the goal you want. In this case, the unit of measurement should be determined according to what you want, for example, by lowering the time, you will be able to enter another category.

The SMART Goal: A—Achievable

The goals set for any project you do have to be achievable since believing in your ability to accomplish them is an important source of motivation. In short, the goals must be ambitious enough to motivate you to give your all to the project. However, you must be careful not to go too far, or you may never reach the end of the tunnel. An achievable goal would answer questions like:

How can I achieve doing the 100-meter pool in 30 seconds if I'm now at 34?

How realistic is the goal given other constraints, such as lack of practice?

A practical example of an achievable goal:

Increase the amount of time you swim and strive to lower those seconds.

The SMART Goal: R—Relevant

There is nothing more useless than setting a goal that is neither meaningful nor contributes to the growth of the objective. Therefore, SMART goals must be relevant to what you do.

Example of a related goal: win a gold medal this year.

The SMART Goal: T—Timely

The T-goal in SMART means setting a time frame and a target date for achieving the goal. Otherwise, you run the risk of getting lost in your projects or procrastinating too much until the work is no longer manageable. However, a target date does not apply to all objectives, such as financial or technical.

A practical example of a timely objective:

You want to organize an event at school. First, you need to find a date when everyone can participate. Then you should set a deadline for the organization, for example, two days before the event. Subsequently, the tasks can be sorted by urgency and processed step by step.

Divide Goals Into Manageable Steps

If you have a big dream to achieve, if you really want to accomplish it, in addition to constancy, you must also divide it into small steps.

To make your big dreams come true, you must divide those big dreams into more manageable parts you can control. Small steps will go a long way. A life-changing dream comes true gradually. After all, the dream of tackling everything at once becomes overwhelming. It's easier to achieve your objectives when you break them down into small goals.

Yes, it's slowed down, but every little accomplishment feels like progress for the big picture. Progress brings you closer to your big dreams. To learn how to reinvent yourself with small goals, you must first figure out the outcomes. Start by thinking about what your dream is, then determine what you need to achieve that outcome. Have a list of the tasks you require to make this dream a reality. Then focus on one task first.

After completing one task, you will need to focus on completing another. Do these tasks daily to complete the reboot process. Make sure you make progress by accomplishing a small feat as motivation to keep going.

Patience Is a Virtue

You have to realize that achieving your dreams will not happen in a day. The reboot process is about taking small steps toward your goals every day without stopping. Also, the process can take years... so patience is essential.

Small Steps Will Help You Go a Long Way

The current reality is the reason why many people fail or often just hope for it without struggling and overcoming difficulties. The media hypes success as if it happened overnight, but it does not. It takes time, and you have to accept it from the beginning so that everything starts to flow without you even realizing it. Let me give you this everyday example: To graduate from school, you started as a child, you will leave practically as an adult, and from there, you go to college, which is at least 4 years. Great achievements take time.

Success takes time, patience, sacrifice, and care, just like raising a child. Children must learn to reinvent themselves by learning to talk, crawl, walk, and understand and process information. Parental guidance can help a child understand things better, similar to how a support group guides them through their dreams. Outside forces that enlighten or hinder a child are similar to strangers helping or hindering sleep.

In the end, spend most of your time on your dreams...to achieve them; you have to prioritize them. You may never achieve them if you always put them second on your priority list.

Flexibility in the Adversity

Life's unpredictable obstacles can often wreck a perfectly sound strategy. An agile person knows how to change course on the fly. A backup plan is an important buffer against a failed primary plan; if all else fails, keep going because there may be an undiscovered solution out there. Perhaps that solution is the answer to how to reinvent yourself.

If life presents other possibilities, don't reject those options. Explore them with an open mind. When the inevitable planning hiccups arise, such as delays and setbacks, respond to the inevitable and address the situation as it unfolds. None of these events are signs of a new beginning. Instead, they are alternative routes to explore.

Life teaches young and old that nothing comes easy. If a path is easy, it also contains fine print that no one wants to accept. The easy road can also lead to a stagnant life... on the other hand, the hard road is always worth taking, and for a reason!

A hard road will strengthen you for the challenges ahead.

Don't try to start over from failure. Never compare or compete with someone who is far away... mistakes are the answer to reinventing yourself. Use it as a guide for current or future remodels.

Track Progress Toward Goals

In addition to setting your goals, it is important to develop a critical path that allows you to monitor your progress, being very clear on the specific objectives for each milestone and the dates you set for achieving them. Rely on this to align your objectives with SMART traits.

Practice Reviewing Progress on Your Goals Weekly

This regular practice will help you ensure your goals are being met.

Read the statement carefully and fill in the blanks by completing the weekly activity information to achieve your goals for the month.

Practical Exercise to Build Your Professional Goals

Go beyond other people's evaluation and expectations of you; whatever makes you live to the fullest, whatever makes you happy, whatever makes you wake up every day, whatever makes you hold on to it is valuable.

The plan is that you work constantly evaluating the professional goals you want to achieve, the personal, sports, growth, your emotions, anything you want, whether it is to get the highest foot up in kung fu or get that dance step, that is key to growth and advancement.

Understanding Resilience

Problems, failures, and setbacks are an inevitable part of our lives. As you mature as a teenager and face more challenges, you also tend to experience more complications.

Learning as a teenager to develop resilience, the ability to adapt, bounce back, and move forward in the face of adversity, can go a long way in helping you excel in your personal and professional life.

The transition to adolescence can be difficult: it is a time of great physical, psychological, and experiential change. Each week brings moments and challenges with new problems to overcome.

Therefore, resilience helps you become increasingly resilient and can equip you with the tools to reduce the impact of negative situations.

What Are the Traits of Resilience?

When you manage to have good doses of resilience, the following traits are more pronounced, all of which can be learned:

Emotional awareness and being able to control emotions.

Confidence that things can be accomplished (self-efficacy).

Empathy for others.

Greater control of impulsivity.

Flexible and accurate thinking.

Optimistic outlook.

Willingness to seek support when needed.

Emotional Awareness and Ability to Regulate Emotions

To be more resilient, you must feel comfortable with your emotions and thoughts and express them appropriately. Understand that you can be in control of them, not the other way around. Consider these tips you can follow:

Name it without blaming: for example, saying "I feel depressed" but not blaming something or someone else for your emotion can reduce the intensity of what you feel.

Pause and focus on one thought. Rushing is the enemy of resilience.

Accept that emotions are not good or bad; they are just that, emotions.

Tips for Learning Impulse Control

We all have the urge to do and say things when we are angry, disappointed, or frustrated. That's normal, and building resilience doesn't mean stopping these processes but learning not to let unproductive impulses overwhelm us. Try this four-step process with you:

Stop and think: This slows down the response.

Take deep breaths: It gives you control and calm.

Before you say anything, think of three possible responses, and choose the most constructive ones.

Respond politely and respectfully so you can listen to yourself better.

Ways to Cultivate an Optimistic Mindset

Learn to be optimistic by encouraging objective thinking around practical issues, such as exams or your future, and encourage yourself to focus on the positive. These exercises help you do just that:

Learn to say, "I can't do it...yet." How we direct words to ourselves affects us. If you can tell yourself you are capable of mastering something, chances are you will eventually get it.

Accept challenges so that you learn. You may feel like you're overwhelmed now, but you'll know how to do better another day.

Doing it is what matters. Many things don't demand perfection, and this includes work and exams. So work to focus on getting it done and not on being perfect.

It's not about seeing the planet through rose-colored glasses, rather, it's about feeling certain that no matter what happens, you will have the ability to cope successfully.

The Value of Thinking in a Timely and Flexible Manner

In a world where the landscape around us is constantly changing, mental flexibility can foster resilience in you. The ability to create a plan B or C and make better decisions eliminates the stress of thinking about what might happen in the future.

These tips can help you think more flexibly and confidently:

Recognize that other people may see things differently. This will motivate you to think about what other people are looking for, which is a useful skill when applying for jobs or dealing with colleagues.

Distinguish between just explaining and actually explaining: for example, is that person forgetting because they are busy and stressed, not because they are inconsiderate?

Realize that it's okay to feel insecure; feeling confident doesn't always guarantee that we are right.

Promote Self-Efficacy to Believe in Yourself

Self-efficacy is a person's confidence in his or her ability to achieve something successfully. This is essential for you to achieve future goals, complete tasks and overcome challenges. How to help improve your self-efficacy by asking questions or making proposals:

> Tell me three things you did well or accomplished last week. How did you feel?

> Tell me three more things you accomplished this quarter that other people have noticed. How do you feel (or did you feel) about it?

Why Resilience Impacts Your Life So Positively

In some cases, throughout our lives, we have to face situations that are beyond our possibilities: it can be a broken relationship, the loss of a loved one, an illness, having to go through certain economic difficulties, the failure of a project in which we placed so much hope... and that's when we need the benefits of resilience.

Difficulties are part of life, and when they occur, they put us in front of two paths: either we fail and give up, or we overcome our circumstances and use them to gain more experience and become stronger from them. This is called resilience.

> Resilient people also criticize themselves, although less than others. Often, these criticisms are aimed at improving certain details of your personality.

> They help you to be more optimistic, to see a ray of light when there seems to be no escape, in short, to be more resolute.

This is because they don't take everything so personally; they are healthier and less stressed.

This attitude is what guarantees success in everything you do, both inside and outside the place where it is done.

They are completely satisfied with their relationships and can analyze all points of failure and correct them as quickly as possible.

A resilient person is less likely to fall into depression... which doesn't mean they shouldn't seek help when they need it.

Now you know what resilience is and the benefits of practicing it.

But before I finish, I want to share my 3 favorite resilient people:

Frida Kahlo was forced to stay in bed after being involved in a car accident. However, in painting, she found the strength and drive she needed to become one of the most famous contemporary painters.

Viktor Frankl, an Austrian psychiatrist, survived several concentration camps. From that experience, he wrote the book that you should read, and many teenagers have on their bedside table, "Man's Search for Meaning," and created the theory of Logotherapy: Having Meaning in Life for Greater Happiness.

Milton H. Erickson had to deal with a series of personal disabilities, the consequences of which resulted in illnesses such as polio. Despite (or perhaps because of) these obstacles, Milton became one of the most effective psychotherapists of all time.

Never mind the obstacles when you have the desire to succeed.

Five Steps to Develop Resilience

Resilience is an inherent capacity in every human being. We are born with it, and it changes as we gain experience and are shaped by our upbringing and culture. Then, in adulthood, some people are very resilient, while others cannot cope with small everyday problems. Adolescence is when you start moving on the road to reach it.

Like all skills, you can enhance them through learning. This way, you can overcome and emerge stronger before negative events occur. With these five steps, you can develop resilience.

Step One: Seek to Be Autonomous

When you are consciously responsible for what happens around you, you also can choose how what you experience affects you. Therefore, generating independence within yourself without the need for constant support will help you see yourself as valid and capable.

Step 2: Live in the Moment

The only moment you have the power to change is now. Neither the past nor the future is within our reach. Excessive hindsight can lead to sadness while worrying about the future can lead to anxiety. Therefore, the state that brings you the most happiness is the present moment. Live each day with optimism and enjoy what you are doing right now. To achieve this, go to the mindfulness section of this book.

Step 3: Endure Frustration

The need to control stresses you out. Letting go and realizing that you are not in control will create an atmosphere of greater uncertainty, but within which you can live more peacefully.

Step 4: Listen to Your Needs

We tend to avoid facing our negative emotions, but they are always valuable and tell us what we need. Sadness or anger is not something we should avoid, but rather listen and give them the space they need.

Step 5: Believe in Yourself

Having a positive view of yourself and knowing you can draw on all your strengths builds resilience. The knowledge you have accumulated over the years will also help you in difficult times.

The key to developing resilience is knowing that your capabilities are valid; through them, you can face situations from an autonomous perspective but always look for the necessary support. Tolerating setbacks, embracing uncertainty, and making room for emotions are tools that will always allow you to come out on top in the face of the problems that arise along the way.

Conclusion

If you got this far, I congratulate you. You have the desire to change, to be a better person, and to face your emotions and the way they control you daily. Surely if you follow the steps, you can go in search of goals, and even when you fail—and I assure you that sometimes you will fail, like all those who are on the road to success—you will know how to get up; you will control your emotions and you will know that it was just a stumble, that tomorrow you will try again. I am grateful for what you have done, I am left with the satisfaction that I could change your life, and you will be someone who sooner or later will reach your goals.

Your New Life Starts Here

Forget everything you lived before reading this book, or better yet, don't forget it; you can see it from a window, like looking at the past, that version you were before, like when you see a person who lost weight and contemplates how he was before and how he is now, or when you see that thin kid with a childish voice and not who you are now with a more adult voice and a body developing into adulthood. In this case, you are already someone else, a young person who is on the way to being different, to do things differently.

When you are sad, remember what you read, start to breathe, reflect, and change where necessary.

If you feel angry about something that didn't go right, before you blow up and respond as you used to, take a moment to breathe, find the right words and respond.

It may get out of control at times. It's like riding a bike; even if you have balance, if you go over a rock and fall, it's because you haven't mastered it yet, but with practice, you will even do somersaults. That's life, jumping and jumping over obstacles.

Review of Key Concepts and Skills

Before closing this book, I want us to remember some of the key concepts that helped us get to where we are now.

In the beginning, I talked about self-regulation, which in simple terms, is to control that emotion unleashed in you, where the volcano wants to explode, and you take a breath before acting, working on it in practice until you regulate it consciously. Then, we went through the emotions. I named the main ones and how they manifest in you, what causes them to show themselves to others, and why you need to evaluate them, especially the low-vibrational ones like anger, sadness, depression, etc.

No emotion is bad; remember, what is bad is how you deal with them. If you let sadness take your body and become depressed, then there is something in your little head working wrong and needs to be restructured, something that I did not mention in the book and is scientifically known as the neuroplasticity of the brain. This characteristic is about how the brain can adapt to different situations and molds itself to new knowledge; it is something that happens all your life. Imagine the brain as a great highway, which at the same time creates new roads according to your needs and what you give it.

In that chapter, I taught you to see emotions from a positive point of view, even those that hurt.

Then, we moved on to the techniques of mindfulness, which is a habit that you can keep in your life forever, taking care of the moment and not thinking so much about the future that gives you anxiety or yesterday that causes you sadness and nostalgia for what was and will never return.

Do the mindfulness exercises, and live in the moment. If you eat, enjoy the bite, feel the taste, how it melts in your mouth, and swallow it. If you walk, look around, look at the people, the cars, the sky, the trees, everything. Combine this with the breath, as I showed you, where I also gave you tools to use the breath even when you are crying, and you feel you can't take it anymore. By breathing in a conscious and controlled way, you can take care of every part of yourself.

Then we talked about problems; maybe until now, you had seen them as the end of the world, but you have realized that problems are part of the game, of the path, and that no matter how ugly everything can be, there is always a solution, a way you assume to solve this problem faster and avoid drowning in a glass of water.

I also talked about goals, using an incredible tool such as SMART goals. Remember to apply this technique in your own way, writing everything you want to achieve in an agenda or an app, and if you categorize it as I taught you, you will achieve it.

Of course, communication was not left out either because I gave you tools and tips to communicate properly with others.

Develop a Personalized Self-Regulation Plan

Everything I showed you in this book with examples and tools was defined so that you can structure it in your way and style, depending on your goals or the emotions you want to regulate. Maybe you are someone who has great sadness, and you took my advice, told your parents, went to the doctor, and they discovered depression.

You may be that guy who gets angry about everything, bursts out in anger, and even breaks things, but you started exercising, and now you control yourself more, even though you know that you have a strong character.

Each of us has our personality and ways of acting in different situations. The plan is that the content I left in this book works for you to adapt it to your way, to what you need, so that in a personalized way, you can take care of yourself, bringing out a better version of yourself and inoculating inside you the good habits and customs of a leader who wants to achieve great goals no matter what comes up along the way. It's all a matter of knowing how to manage yourself, growing, bringing out a better version of yourself, striving every day, and, most importantly, believing.

I know that school is difficult and that there are cruel classmates; in childhood and adolescence you have no filter to say things, they hurt you, and they make you feel bad and insecure. But let me tell you that no matter what they say, one day you won't care, and you will know that it was just "kid" stuff. When you learn to believe in yourself, everything others said will slip away.

Scan the QR code to access the link to download your bonus!

Printed in Great Britain
by Amazon

38037018R00057